Connect graphic design and print

Connect
graphic design
and print

The ultimate tool for saving time and money for Packaging / Label Designers, Business Start-up, Packaging Technologist, Artwork Approvers and Print Buyers

Anthony Baptiste

Twitter: @thegraphicarc

www.thegraphicarc.com

ISBN 978-1-8383703-2-9

www.Thegraphicarc.com

Author Bio

In an almost 30-year career, Anthony has been involved in the commercial print industry—from high-value international wine and spirits label stock to the dizzying world of fast-moving consumer goods (FMCG) packaging of key multinational players. He has worked on print presses, made printing plates, and worked in pre-press (repro). He has worked predominately in flexographic printing but also has involvement in screen, digital, and offset print. The list of substrates he has worked with includes paper, plastic, card, metallise film/paper and rubber. His knowledge covers not only the back-end of printing but also the front office in order processing, works quotations and sales executive. His experience spans both sides of the Atlantic Ocean and four printers, producing work sold in more than thirty-seven countries.

Table of Contents

A personal forward

Let me start by saying that the following sections are not taught as a single cohesive unit in any design class for labels and or packaging. This is because most graphic design courses don't believe it is necessary beyond the basics.

The true power of design is the creativity involved in problem-solving. I have written this book because I foresee the evolution of design as a complete tool. The objective for which is to allow the designer to deeply realise their creation. To do so requires a foundation in understanding of print and related techniques. This will endow the designer or artwork contact person with more control of the design from concept to retail shelf and through to marketing.

For print buyers, artwork approvers, artwork buyers, and packaging technologists, an understanding of the complete process is essential. This ensures that you are knowledgeable about what you see on screen, understand the issues in printing, packing, and what is received as a final product. With this knowledge, you will be able to demand higher standards from your designer and improved outcomes with the print company and packer/ bottler.

The aims of this handbook:

To bridge the gaps between design and print.

To teach the integration of print fundamentals into planning for graphic design.

To broaden and deepen a learner's knowledge and understanding of graphic design elements as they relate to print.

To assist artwork approvers in recognising critical print element requirements and cost.

To boost the capabilities of artwork buyers in writing detailed and accurate briefs.

To outline the important questions to ask about graphic design prior to printing.

What will you gain from using this handbook?:

Graphic designers can enter the packaging design market with greater confidence.

Packaging designers will improve their post design understanding.

Print buyers in businesses can be certain of what they will receive as a finished label or package.

Artwork approvers will be assured that they can spot all the critical elements of their package or label before it goes to print.

Business start-ups who are getting into or have some experience with print will gain wide-ranging knowledge of the packaging and print industries reducing cost.

Product technologists who have either migrated to their position or those fully trained will expand the scope and depth of their working print knowledge.

In reality, all these areas overlap greatly, so a good read-through is essential.

Key questions for your printer:

When can I set my print date?

This needs to be done as early as possible to reserve your print date.

🚫 **Issues**: Base materials such as film, paper, or special ink may need to be bought in.

🏆 **Hot Tip**: Consider booking your print date even before you start the design process. If you are selling into supermarkets and fail to make delivery dates, you could lose shelf space.

What is your minimum order quantity?

Work this out for what your product needs plus additional for the packer. The packer will need to set up, stop and start the film for the packing machine. This means there will be a small amount of working / wastage to be added. Approximate 1-3% on runs.

🚫 **Issues**: The minimum order may be an order value, an amount of material, or labels. Confirm with the packer what excess material they need. There will always be a small amount wastage.

🏆 **Hot Tip**: The minimum order may be in meters, kilos / tonnes, or impressions for flexible packaging such as film. Number of labels for printed labels. Check with your printer and match with your packaging / labelling needs. Companies may typically run 5-10% over (extra print) or under (short of the amount ordered. Always have more packaging than products. No one wants to end up with unpacked products.

Do you have the base stock material or similar in stock?

Some materials are standard while others may be specialised. Is your material in stock as a standard stock item? If a special material is required, check that it can be delivered on time for your print and or delivery dates.

🚫 **Issues**: Special material costs more as there are also MOQs (minimum order quantities) to your print supplier.

🏆 **Hot Tip**: Ask your packer/ bottler if they have used your packaging material and acquired a test reel. Test and agree on the label material and adhesive for your bottle or package.

What is the maximum number of colours you can print?

Depending on your product / commercial printer, they may print a min of 1, 2, 3, 4, up to 8 or 10 colours. Some products may have up to 12 applications, which could include embossing and foiling.

🚫 **Issues**: Ensure that the number of colours plus any varnishes and effects can be printed by your commercial printer.

🏆 **Hot Tip**: Ask your commercial printer what is the maximum number of colours that they can print. Then have your designer design around this.

What special effects do you offer?

Can they do special effects such as gloss, matt, or satin varnishes? Can they emboss or affect a tactile varnish? Do they have glow-in-the-dark or temperature-responsive inks? Be careful of fluorescent inks as they are significantly more expensive and have a shorter shelf life on a product.

🚫 **Issues**: Special material / effects / inks cost more. There are also MOQs (minimum order quantities) for your print supplier to consider.

🏆 **Hot Tip**: If you are a new start-up, consider not having every special effect on offer. Very often, 'less is more' in design. Do plan for them in a staged process for when business moves in a positive direction.

What core sizes can you supply?

Most packaging that is supplied to the packer on a reel uses standard-size cores. Most standard-size cores will fit on the packer's equipment. It is, however, important to know which ones will fit the packing or labelling equipment.

Issues: Not every standard-size core will fit on the flexible packaging packer equipment. The same is true for your labelling company.

Hot Tip: Check with your packer and labelling company for the correct core sizes that they accept. Will the printer supply the MOD (maximum outside diameter) needed for a finished reel by the bottler / packer?

Key questions for your commercial packer and or labelling company:

What finished sizes can you use in your process?

Packing equipment is sold as a unit, then various attachments are added to pack specific products. The same is true for labelling and box folding automated equipment. Relay this to the printer and confirm any conflicts.

🚫 **Issues**: Your chosen packer may not be able to do every size or configuration.

🏆 **Hot Tip**: Before beginning your design, always check the specs of each stage in your product construction process. Designing to fit the process is always less costly in the long run.

Can you meet my packing and delivery date?

Can I have my product packed by X date? Packing dates should be pre-booked as with print dates. Allow at least two weeks between the two dates as things can go wrong. Does this sync with your delivery date for your contracted shelf space?

Do you provide an overprinting service?

Most packers / labelers / bottlers offer some or limited overprint services.

🚫 **Issues**: Colours are usually limited to black or red. Other companies offer laser or foil blocking.

🏆 **Hot Tip**: Before beginning your design, always check the specs amount and placement of any overprint areas. Also, check the text sizes and styles available to you. Always check the tolerance, i.e., the amount of movement allowed by the overprint device before it encroaches onto the design. This could be as small as 2 mm or as high as 10mm. Check if the overprint is affected by varnishes and what kinds.

Will your label stick to and stay my product?

🚫 **Issues**: All adhesives (glues) are not created equal. Every adhesive has a specific purpose and life cycle.

🏆 **Hot Tip**: Always check that their adhesives will meet your needs. It might make sense to purchase larger quantities to get better prices. However, whether glue will be at its best after storage, sale, and kitchen time is a great question to ask. Always check the lifespan of any adhesive used. Knowing it's storage conditions is important.

Key questions for your graphic designer:

Do you have experience creating packaging or labels?

Many graphic designers can create beautiful packaging, but experience goes a long way in ensuring that what you pay for in-studio is possible in your chosen print method and chosen printer.

🚫 **Issues**: Print is a very technical process and what looks great on screen is not always applicable to commercial print processes. It can be very costly if labelling and packaging issues are not solved during the design process.

🏆 **Hot Tip**: Use an experienced design house or this manual for guidance.

How deep is your knowledge of legal information on pack / label

In every way, your business is responsible for the information and images used on your product. In effect, every package can be interpreted as a contract with its purchaser and laws of the countries within which it is sold. You are legally bound to the safety of the product as well as its graphics and text.

🚫 **Issues**: There are legal requirements surrounding image use, size, and even what it represents. Font sizes used in text required by law are strict. Research this or have a competent person design for you.

🏆 **Hot Tip**: Check the copyright of all images and fonts (text styles) used in your packaging and labelling. Many fonts are free for personal and not commercial use. Check. Check. Check. Barcode sizes and colours are also a pinch point.

Is there access to a colour-accurate printed proof?

This is the closest digitally printed representation of what will be printed on a printing press.

🚫 **Issues**: Because of the variety of substrates (printing materials), desktop printers, and monitors, there is a necessity to be relatively certain of your print outcome before cash outlay to the printer.

🏆 **Hot Tip**: Have your graphic designer contact your printer to clarify the file formats needed. Then, ask for a digital proof (hard copy) from their repro company or plate provider. These are best viewed in natural daylight or a room with daylight bulbs. Where possible attend important press passes. Remember time is money. To translate at least one person attending the pass should be a final decision maker. On press passes are hands on and cannot be done remotely.

Can you supply industry-compatible file formats?

Within the commercial printing field, almost every printer will use industry-standard software to create files (artwork).

🚫 **Issues**: Graphic design formats can be an issue when it goes to the printer or repro house. Repro houses prepare designs for the final print. You may have to return to your graphic designer after signing off your artwork. There could be a fee for converting files.

🏆 **Hot Tip**: Check that the file formats you are given align with what your printer and or repro house requires.

Commercial print basics:
A guide for graphic designers and the rest of us

The critical importance of understanding flexographic printing:

In this section, I will in large part address Flexo (flexographic) print, which is the most widely used, often misunderstood, and at times a challenging form of printing.

This is the form of printing that you are most likely to encounter in your hunt for a printer. This printing technique is used on sachets, plastic bags, corrugated board, card boxes, hang tags, neck collars, cartons, fabrics, film-covered packs, such as yogurt pots, and labels, to name a few. Although in the early 2000s experts were writing off flexo printing, the advent of new plate technologies, screening types and servo driven machines has seen the flexographic printing grow from strength to strength. In the coming sections, I will lay out some of the challenges. With this knowledge, your decision-making process will improve tremendously.

Flexo techniques should be considered for all designs. This is because various components of a product may be printed flexo. for example, a bottle of wine. The corrugated carton may be offset printed, while the label and neck tag is flexo printed, and the website and social media are in a digital web format. It may also be the case that you are starting out small and so digital is the most cost-effective option. You could run the risk of losing loyal customers when you have outgrown digital print and need to move to flexo print because it is more cost-effective on medium to larger print runs. There could be a dramatic change in the look and feel of the package or label due to the change to flexo.

The aim is that the communication touchpoints must all have the same look and feel. Therefore, there must be an understanding of flexo, which is both versatile and challenging. That is to say, if you can design for flexo, you can design for anything of the other print available print methods.

The first thing to understand is that flexography print requires printing plates. This is also true of every other print method apart from digital print. Think of a plate as somewhat similar to the potato stamps you created as a child. Each stamp or plate prints one colour in the flexo process.

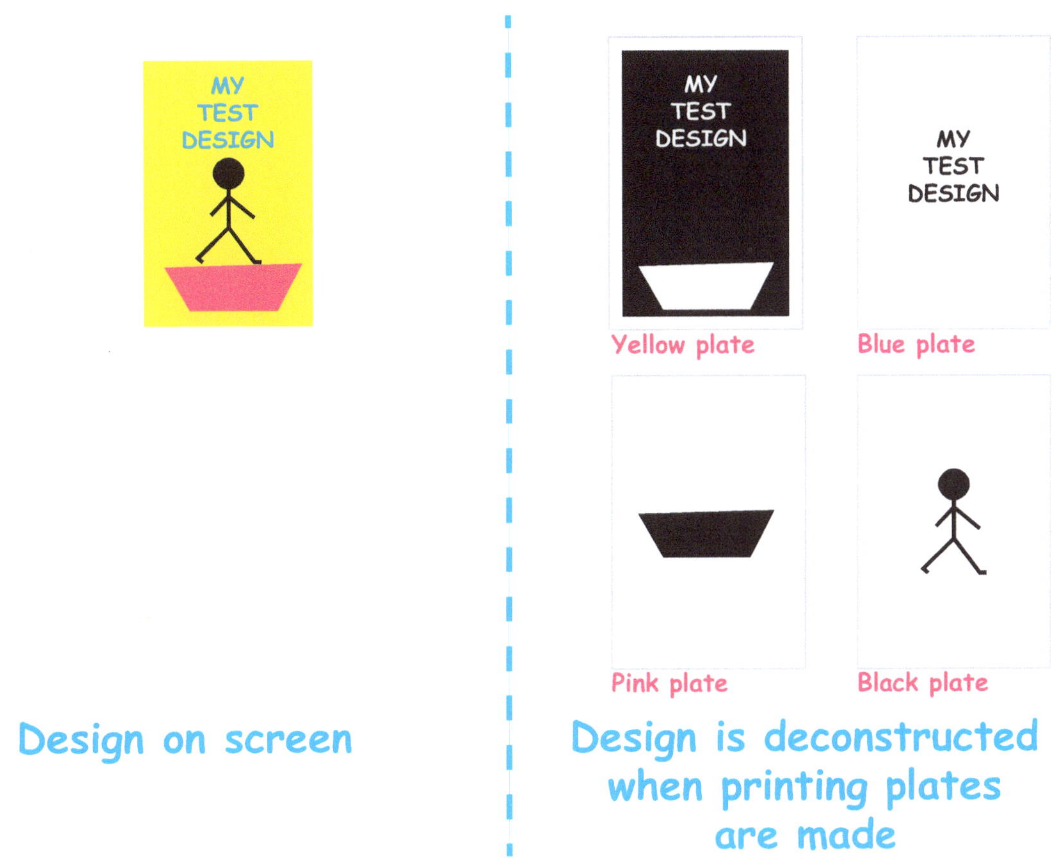

Illustration 1. Each colour in an image is converted to a printing plate of photopolymer (flexible rubber-like) material.

Flexographic machine types:

Type 1: Printing stations are arranged around a central drum, and the printed material, film, or paper is pulled through the printing press. This is called a central impression press. It is typically used for flexible packaging, e.g., plastic bags, sachets. See illustration 2 below.

Flexographic Machines Type 2: Printing stations are arranged sequentially in a line. This is called inline printing. It is typically used for adhesive labels, corrugated material, cardboard boxes, and cartons. See illustration 2 below.

Ok, now that you have an idea of the print process, let us look at the key challenges facing flexo.

Looking at the illustration above, basic colour problems leap out. Keep in mind the print sequence illustrated above. For example: should we print blue text onto the yellow box, the text will appear green and not blue. Should we print the pink boat over the yellow box, then the result will be an orange boat. That's basic colour mixing. The black printed onto the yellow causes no problems. This is because the black is strong enough not to be affected. This problem is solved in Illustration 1. Notice the cut-out areas in the yellow plate. There are cut-outs for the pink and blue. There is no cut-out for the black. This group of images of the various printing plates is called colour separation.

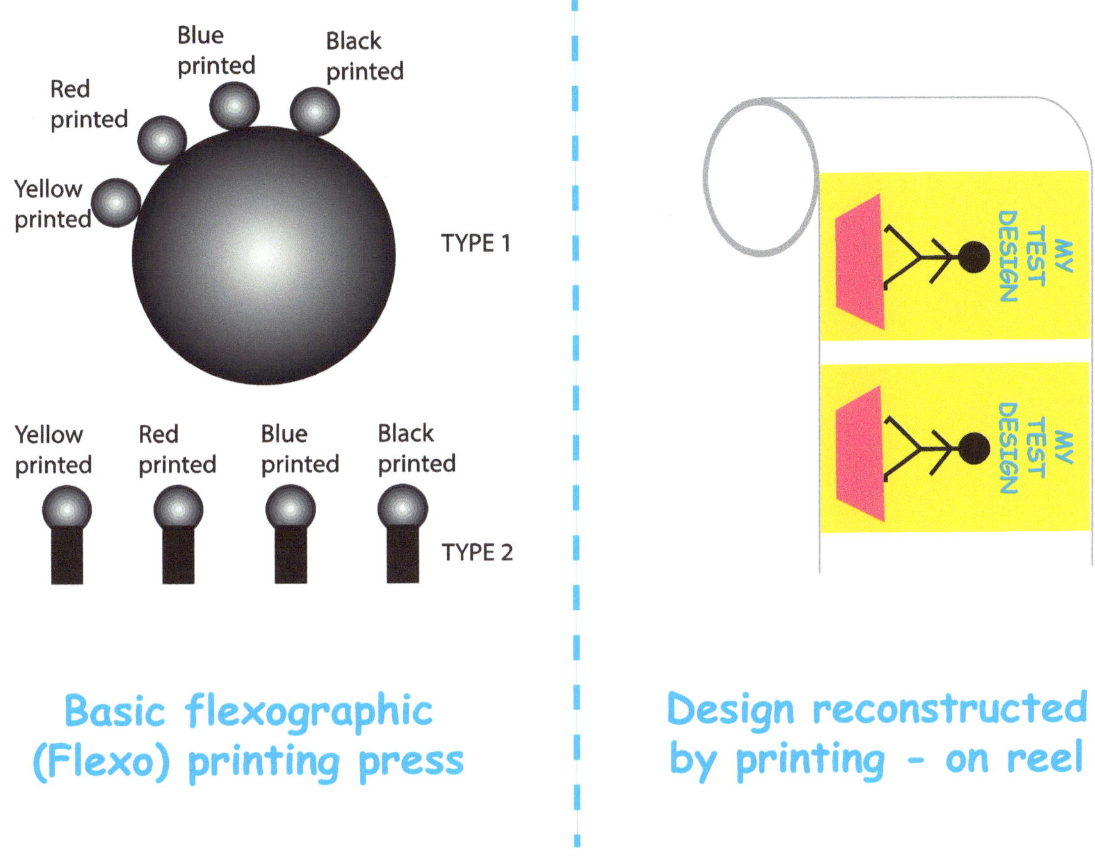

Basic flexographic (Flexo) printing press

Design reconstructed by printing – on reel

Illustration 2. Each plate is trimmed to the circumference of the print cylinder. The plate is then mounted to the cylinder using double-sided adhesive tape. Each printing plate prints one colour until the image is completed. **Retain this idea of the trimmed printing plate.**

Life would be perfect if all the plates stayed exactly in place as the press ran. Unfortunately, that's not the case as there are very small movements between each plate. The amount of movement can create a small gap as small as .1mm that needs to be adjusted for as this could lead to unwanted white gaps. This is called misregistration. See left side image below in illustration three.

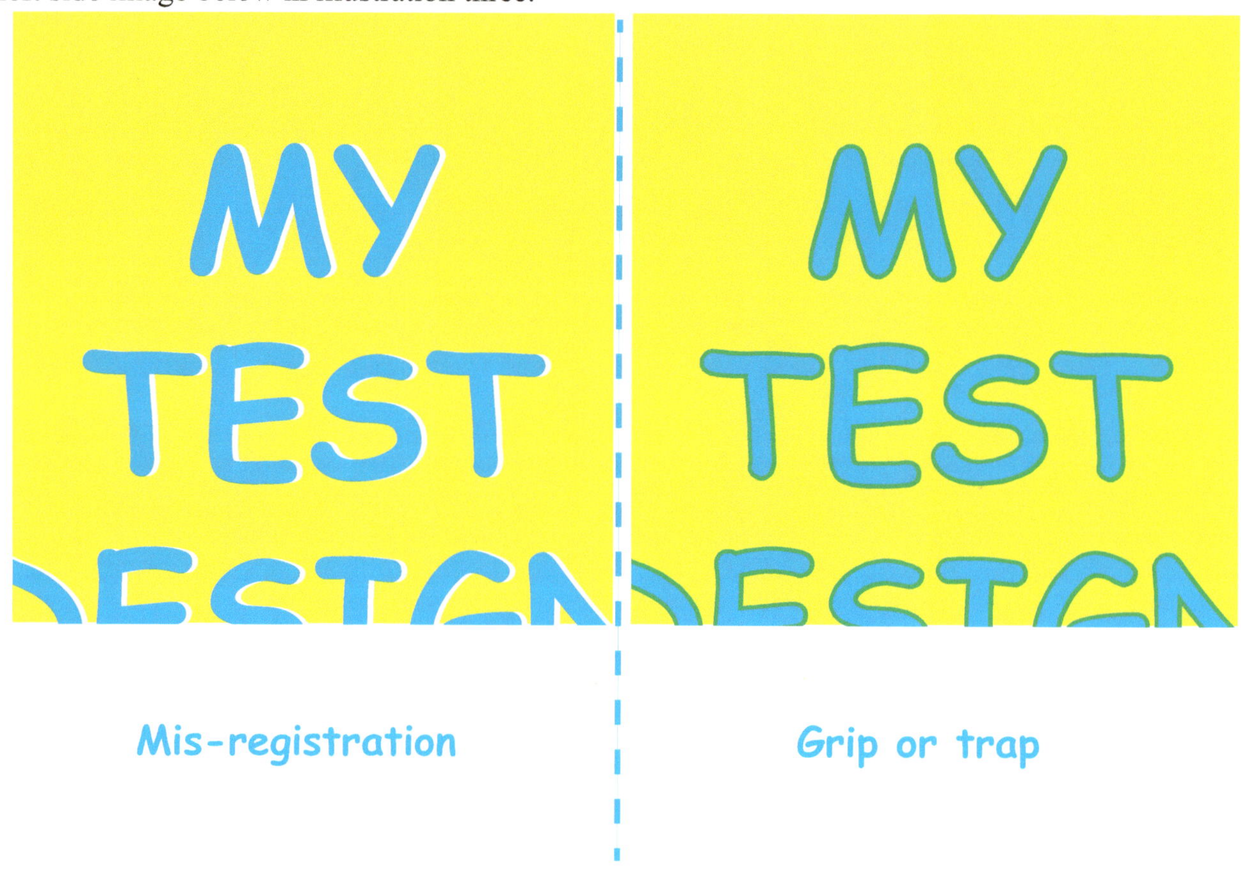

Illustration 3. Left shows the unwanted white. Right shows grip to compensate for any minor movement in the print run.

To counter the effect of misregistration, there is a compensation made called grip or trap. See illustration three above. Grip is achieved by choking or spreading one colour under or into another. Depending on how you see it. Has the yellow been spread under the blue, or has the yellow been choked under the blue? The generic terms are grip or trap.

So, what's this got to do with anything? Great question! Well, notice that where the grip is, there is a bit of colour mixing. The edge of the blue has turned green. This part of the print process that compensates for these small movements is called Repro or pre-press work. This is when the Repro or Pre-press professional prepares the files for print.

This is what the designer and print buyer must consider for every colour in every design presented. *When it's gripped for print, will I like the result?* is the question to ask yourself. Of course, a grip or trap of .15mm is an average standard, which is quite small and will not present an issue on 97% of designs on paper or film. On corrugated board, it could be 1 or 2mm.

How to get around this? Well, we could place a white outline around the blue text. A line thick enough so that even with small movements, the blue and yellow never touch. Voila! No green. Before you break out the celebration, there is the question, what if my blue text or graphic is really small, for example, with ingredients text? A white outline, in this case, may make the small blue artwork appear a bit blurry. The text or art is also too small for a grip. In these cases, consider accepting that the text will be green instead of blue or consider making the text black or another colour that may not interact with yellow, such as brown. These are examples of designing around a potential print problem. Consideration of the print process gives greater power to the designer or buyer.

The same thought process should be followed for every colour interaction. This means that you are designing for the print process. Creating graphics in this way gives the creator more control of the final outcome. The same issues are not exactly the same for offset and digital print. Think of digital print as an enlarged desktop printer. Offset has a higher degree of accuracy as the design is first put onto a transfer blanket from the plates. When all colours have been added, the complete design is added to the print material. This is how cans are printed as an example.

🚫 **Issues**: Colours can clash

🏆 **Hot Tip**: Therefore, wherever colours touch or overprint each other for flexo print, consider the effect of the overlap/ grip and design accordingly. Find out the print parameters of your client's printing company.

Understanding flexo plates and print outcomes:

 We previously read that flexo plates are made from a rubber-type material called photopolymer. So, why do we need this information as anyone in the many touchpoints of design, approval, and print? This is because every design that goes to the edge of the cutter/ die/ keyline may be affected by what you are actually printing.

Illustration 4. Each images is stepped (moved and copied) and repeated (moved and copied). Step is used to reference the the process of moving the copied images across the print web. Repeat refers to the copying of images along the print web.

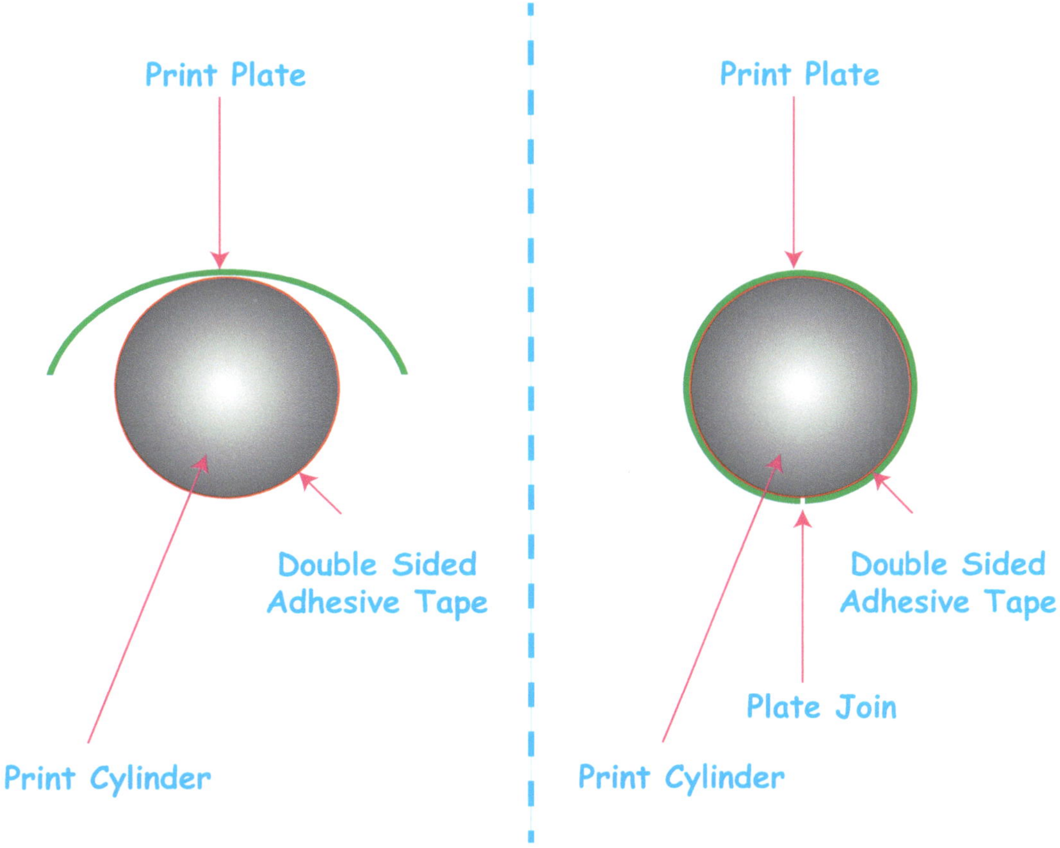

Illustration 4A. All the plates are cut and joined. Only plates with print on the perimeter of the design in the running direction of the printing press may be negatively impacted. This results in loss of colour shown as a white strip. If the gap is the white plate and the colour that overprints the gap will be translucent / transparent.

🚫 **Issues**: Keep in mind that the plate must come to an end.

🏆 **Hot Tip**: It may seem obvious, but every plate is a specific size. Likewise, unless the plate is often several images on one plate, where they join directly to each other, the print will be ok. Note: jointed around the printing web. It is where these joins occur that has to be strongly considered when designing, approving, or buying a print. The illustration below shows the same image stepped and repeated (copied) to make a working plate.

Print that touches the boundary of the design:

When a design is created where it bleeds off (ink touches the parameter of the design), the designer, print buyer, approver, or technologist must be conscious of both the plate join and the web direction. The plate is trimmed to the circumference of the print cylinder (see Illustration 4 above). Being conscious of this particular type of design and its correlation to plates will help you manage your expectations of the final print outcome.

Illustration 5. Here the images are stepped three times and repeated twice. Making Six images per plate. As per image 4 above. Notice the vertical white gap. This is where the plates are cut and joined. The join creates a natural gap

Labels: So what if this were a butt-cut label?

A butt-cut label is when a label is cut from the web on press with no gaps between the labels. In other words, the cut areas butt or meet each other. In Illustration 5, the cut will fall in the white area of a butt cut. This is because the die-cut occurs after every image. However, there is the possibility of a white strip as this is where the plate is joined. This results in the first and third images having a bit of undesirable white on the vertical edge where the image print bleeds off.

🚫 **Issues**: Unwanted white on the edge of the label.

🏆 **Hot Tip**: Design with a white border, and the problem is solved. Another idea is to have vertical stripes in the design so that the plate join naturally falls between the gaps in the design. These options are only considered for the colours that will touch the ends of the plates. In the design of illustration 5, it is only the gold colour / plate that is affected. One more option is to use an engraved sleeve. This is a laser-etched rubber cylinder or sleeve. As this is etched over the entire cylinder, there is no join to consider. The cost of a laser may be four times the cost of a polymer plate, so a balance must be struck.

Labels: So what if this were a die-cut label?

A die-cut label is when a label is cut from the web on press with regular-sized, naturally occurring gaps between each label. This leaves a gap of waste material. Look at the example below. The plate join will naturally fall into the gaps so that there is no unwanted white space on the label.

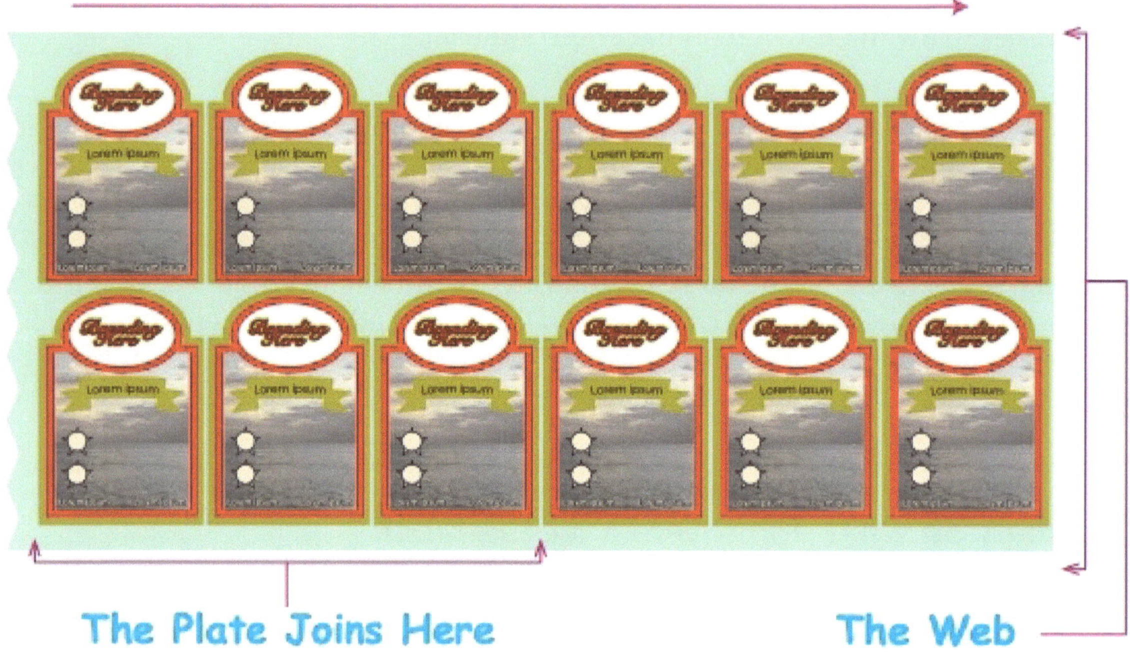

Illustration 6. Die-cut labels. The green web colour represents the white backing paper of the label reel.

Issues: Cutter type not communicated.

Hot Tip: Before starting a label design, confirm with the buyer and or printer if the design is a die or a butt cut.

Flexible plastic packaging: "Plastic bags" by nature are butt cuts

Flexible packaging is supplied to the packer on rolls / reels. They are not cut on the press as with some labels (like butt cuts) but are separated in the packing plant. Now, take a look at the illustration below and think about what you have already read about flexo plate joins and butt cuts.

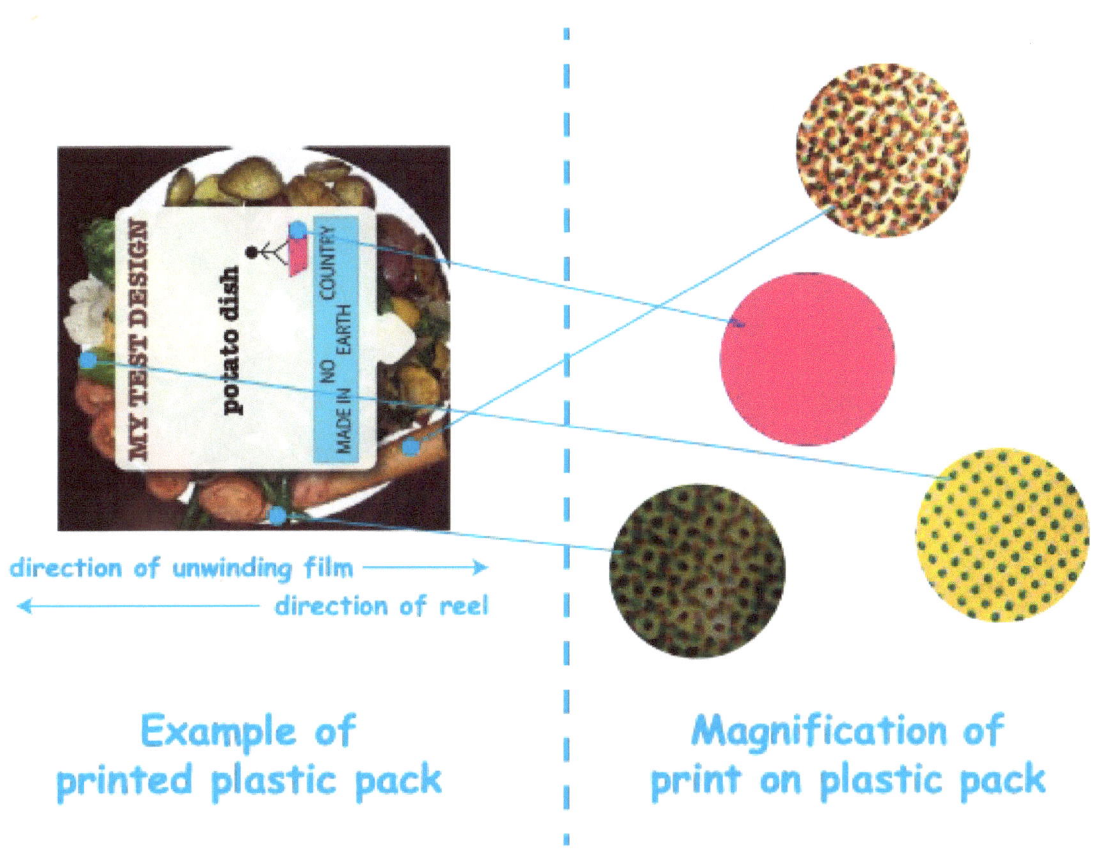

Illustration 7. The image on the left is printed with four colours. These primary colours are called CMYK Colours. C= cyan (blue) M= magenta (red) Y= yellow and K= black.

Notice how different areas are made up of different percentages of dots. There is no green ink that makes up the green colours. Instead, it is the percentage of cyan (blue) that is overprinting the yellow ink. Orange and every other colour will be mixed similarly. Notice how the pink boat is 100%. So, how do we get to this dot stage? A bit of software kit converts what appears to be flat colour into a series of dots on a printing plate. As above, these dots percentages, printed as individual inks in the printing process, mixing the colours in this way results in a great variety of colours.

Back to the issue of how the plates for the above design are cut to wrap around the print cylinder. Review Illustration 5. The four plates will be joined every three repetitions, leaving a white gap. This means that only the middle pack will be perfect. Aside from the white gap, there is the issue of four sets of colours caused by four differently cut plates. So, how do we work around this? Below are two possible options.

Illustration 8. Example on the left makes the image area smaller than the actual cut size along the reel. The design is four colours. On the right side, the image has been made smaller and a solid colour bar added to the design. The design now becomes five colours. You will see these two options on every supermarket shelf.

Take some time to look at printed packs the next time you are in the supermarket to see if you can spot either of these two solutions.

So, there is now a logical question screaming to be answered. Why is there no cut gap in the solid colour filler bar? The solution is to move the first half of the bar at the top of the pack to the very bottom of the third pack. This is done during the repro / prepress stage of preparing the artwork for print. What this does is to make three bars of the same size on the plate. Remember that the images constantly repeat on the cylinder so that this method works. See Illustration 9 below. If we were to cut a plate in the logical place, we would end up with four bars: two bars of the same size, plus two bars fifty percent the width of the widest bars. This will result in a wanted white gap. An alternative is to use stripes of the CMYK instead of the bar as long as all colours have a natural gap.

Illustration 9. Notice how the 'split / filler' bar has been moved to create three equal-size bars. Each bar between packs represents the top on one pack and the bottom of the next pack. Also, note views of the colour breakdown and mixes. Also review Illustration 10 below.

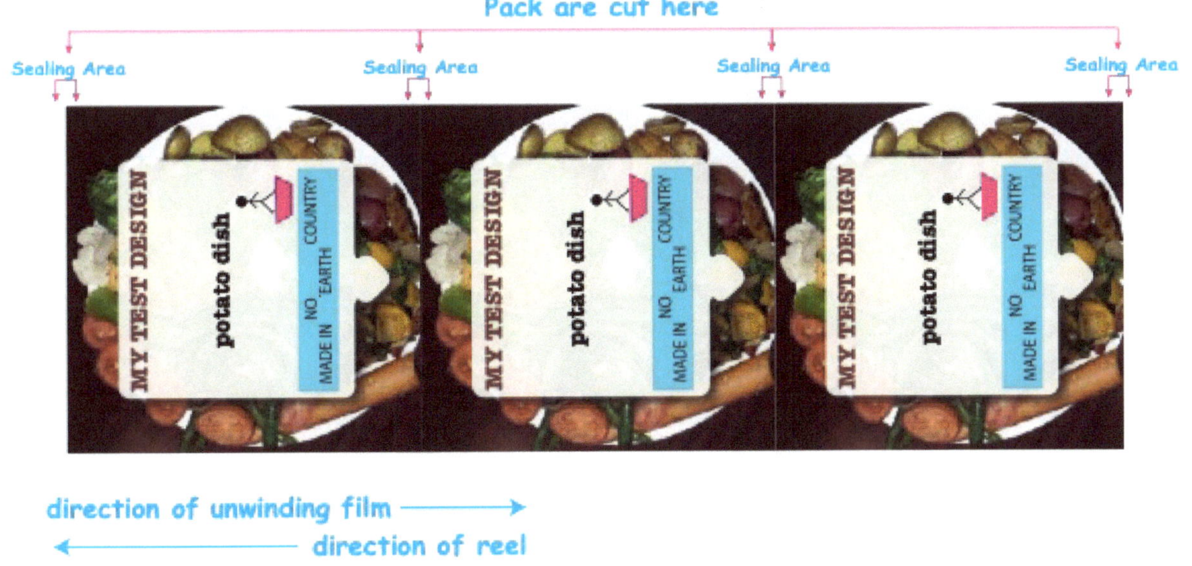

Considerations in the packing and sealing process

Illustration 10. Most graphic packaging design is taught as if each design is set up to print as a single item. However, it is very rarely the case for most other print methods. It is much cheaper commercially for a printer to print multiple images at the same time.

What becomes important is to make a study of the steps that follow on from the initial design. The study includes not only the design as a single unit but how the design and its layout are affected by both printing and packing / labelling process.

Now that you know that these are potential solutions, you could use them in your design setup to avoid any unwanted white. These fixes also work with Pantone® / spot colours that bleed off the pack.

Direction Of Travel Of The Web
(Print Direction)
EYEMARK / EYE BLOCK TRACK
PACK CUTS HERE
PACK CUTS HERE
PACK SLITS HERE
PACK SLITS HERE
EYEMARK / EYE BLOCK
The Web
GREEN REPRESENTS THE SUBSTRATE
Lorem
ipsum dolor
sit amet,
Lorem
ipsum dolor
sit
SEED PACK
12345

Illustration 11. Typical flexible (plastic) packaging laid out on the web.
The bar actually offered two solutions. The first is to save the appearance of a white gap because of the plate cut. The second is to create a consistent, uniformed pack appearance.

As we have seen, labels may be die-cut or butt-cut on the press. For cartons, these are generally stamped out of the printed design from sheets. For flexible plastic packs, this is not usually the case. A printed reel as shown in illustration 11, notwithstanding any plate gaps or unwanted white space, still has a major issue that good design can solve.

Are there any issues that you can see resulting from the cutting process? Well, there should be none but only in theory. In the actual running on a packing line there could be a variation of between zero and plus / minus three millimetres movement on top-quality equipment. This could result in three millimetres of the printed image appearing in the top or bottom of an individual pack as they are filled and separated.

🚫 **Issues**: Plate joining is an absolute issue. The plates must be joined at some point.

🏆 **Hot Tip**: Plates can be joined anywhere at 90 degrees to the running direction of the web. Apply this concept from the idea in Illustration 9. Where the images may be moved to allow a 'natural join' (no print) as opposed to a butt join (through print).

🚫 **Issues**: Any area that is cut, joined, or slit has the potential of having unwanted print from its neighbouring plates or losing print that is maybe cut off in the process.

🏆 **Hot Tip**: Note the bottom two images are set up to be unmasked / extended to create a clean printed slit. The print has been pulled in from the edge on the left and right because the flower shapes on the bottom of the left images are not identical to the shapes on the top of the right image. The gap also allows for any slight movement of the blade / cut as the pack is sealed.

So, what is reverse text? It is when the text has been cut out of a colour so that we can see either the white material or the white or other colour ink below. On-screen, colours often appear solid, but if they have been printed as process colours (CMYK) or a percentage of a solid colour (Pantone®), then they are not solid but made up of dots.

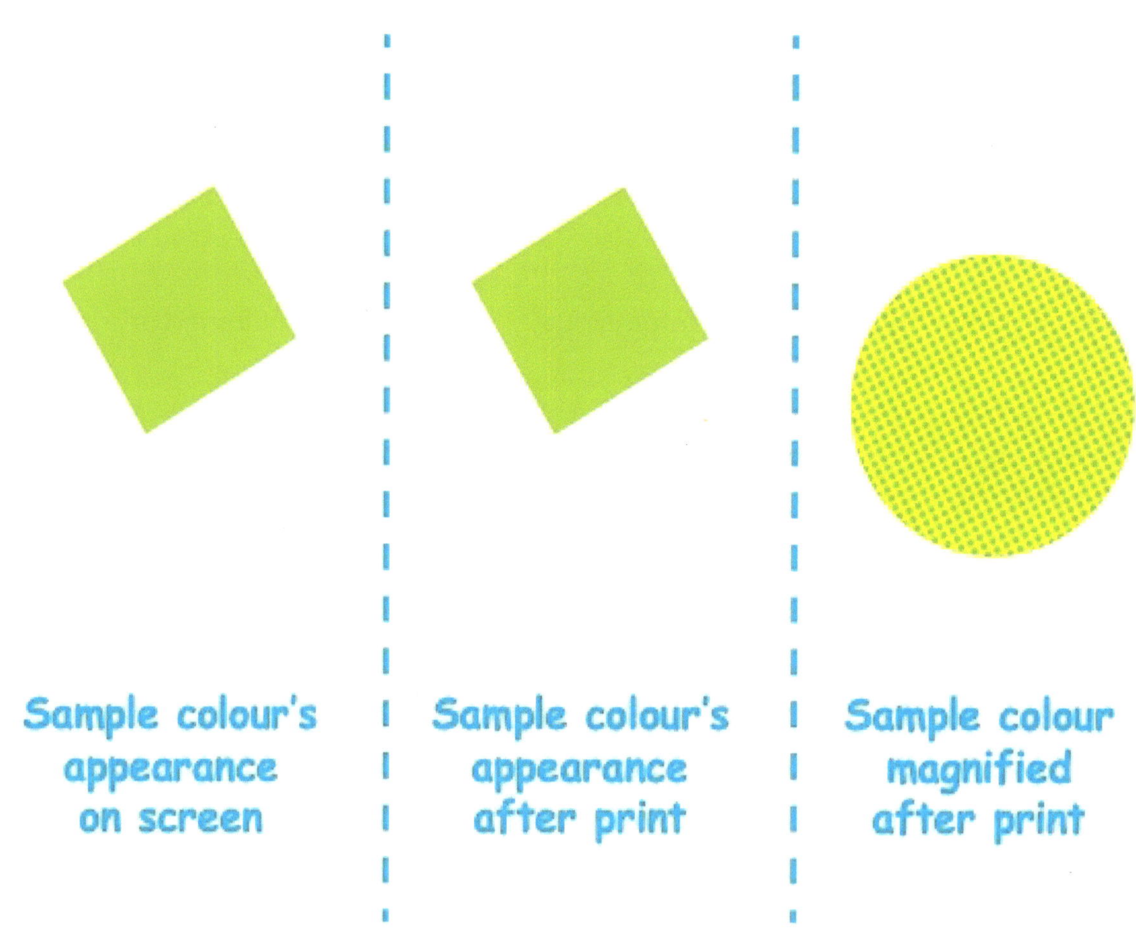

Illustration 11. In the example above, the green is made up of two colours: cyan (blue) and yellow.

What do we have so far? We understand that when using process colours, the colour are generally first broken down into dots. This is the same for a colour percentage of a spot Pantone® colour. We know from earlier that some small but noticeable movements of the plates can occur on the press. So, what happens when there are small movements that encounter the reverse type?

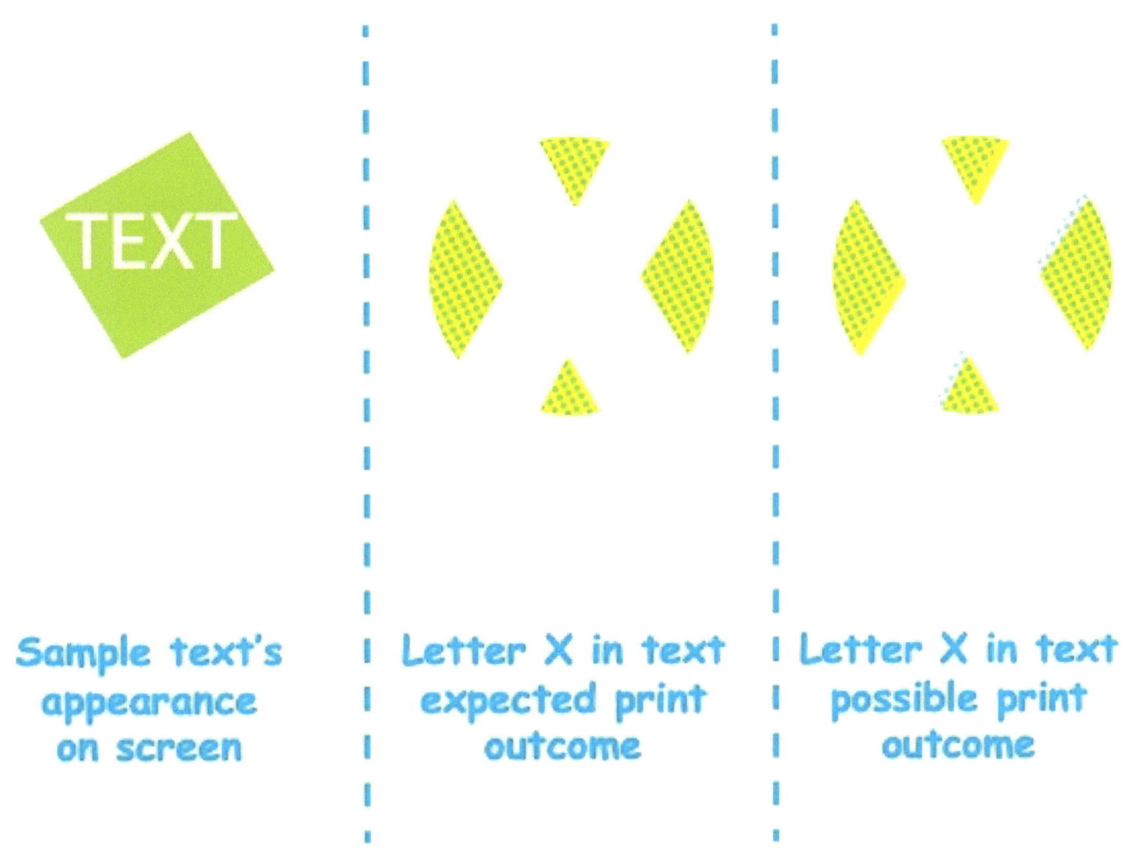

Illustration 12. The screen view vs. perfect print vs. possible print view

Illustration 12 shows the possible outcomes from the print. From the above, we can determine two things. One is that if we have quite small text, then the encroaching colour may fill the gap and cause the reversed text to be illegible. Two is that when we create a tint or percentage of a colour, then that will be in the form of dots. There will be no smooth lines depending on the gaps between the dots, as seen on a screen or monitor. This will explain why on some prints, there may be a black line surrounding the white reverse text. The black line creates a smooth (100% colour) printed line and hides any minor shifts in print.

⊘ **Issue**: Reverse text: Text where the surrounding colour(s) form the shape of the text.

🏆 **Hot Tip**: Use reverse script and serif-styled text where the smallest areas are above a .23mm thickness. Use reverse sans serif text 8 point and above when multiple inks form the reverse colour. Add your own black or dark solid colour (100%) line to your own liking so that the design is printed as you imagined. For example, if you are working with a green colour as above, then finish with a 100% thin cyan line. This prevents the use of black, which can sometimes appear harsh or alter the mood of the design. Another method is to place a thin yellow line that 'shifts' the blue dots away. This compensates for the movements in the blue dots so that they do not encroach into the white area. Of course, this must be a very thin line in the region of .07 as process yellow on its own will not provide high contrast or legibility These are general tips, so always check with your printer for their guidelines.

Reverse text: Across multiple colour areas

So, what is reverse text? It is when the text has been cut out of the background printed colour ink.

A-design

B-keyline added - black

C-design print possibility

D-keyline added - purple

Illustration 13. Top left (A) illustrates reverse text across 2 colour areas. Top right (B) shows a black outline on the reverse text. The purple spot colour is added to the reverse text on the bottom right (D) image. Image C indicates possible outcomes with a shift in plates.

The images B and D of illustration 13 show two solid colour outlines that provide a solution to a possible issue shown on image C. The line should ideally be one solid colour. The colour chosen should be the one that best complements the design.

So, why does screen colour change to dots or not?

All colours appear to be smooth on screen. Take a look at your screen under a magnifying glass, and you will see it is actually made up of red, blue, or green dots or lines. This gives you screen resolution. Screen resolution is just another way of describing how smooth a line is on screen—the higher the screen resolution, the smoother the edge. On-screen, colours are mixed by emitting red, green, and blue light. This mix of RGB creates all the colours on the screen. RGB is not used in print, and no electronically formatted design for print should be supplied in RGB. In print, CMYK or Pantone® or both are used.

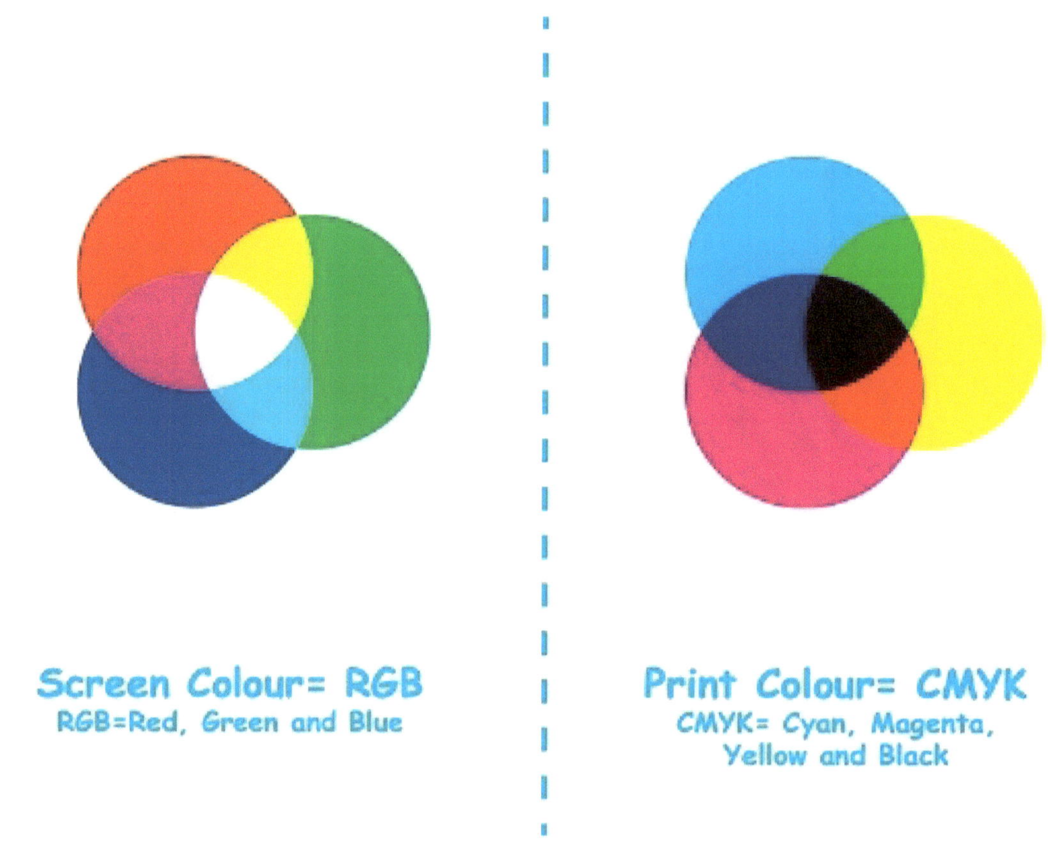

Illustration 14. Basic colour mixing on screen and on a printing press. The absence of RBG colours is black on screen. The mixture of all CMYK colours create black in print.

On a press, we cannot mix CMYK colours as we do in a mixing can. Colour mix is achieved by a bit of clever technology. Specialised software creates screens (dots) by breaking the colour components into a dot equivalent percentage of the colour required. These dots are then printed using ink at 100% colour. The simplest form of viewing this dot-creating process is the monotone. A monotone is when an image is made from percentages of dots of a single colour, usually black. A single colour (spot colour) is better printed from one of the lighter, equivalent shades available in the Pantone® range of colours. www.pantone.com.

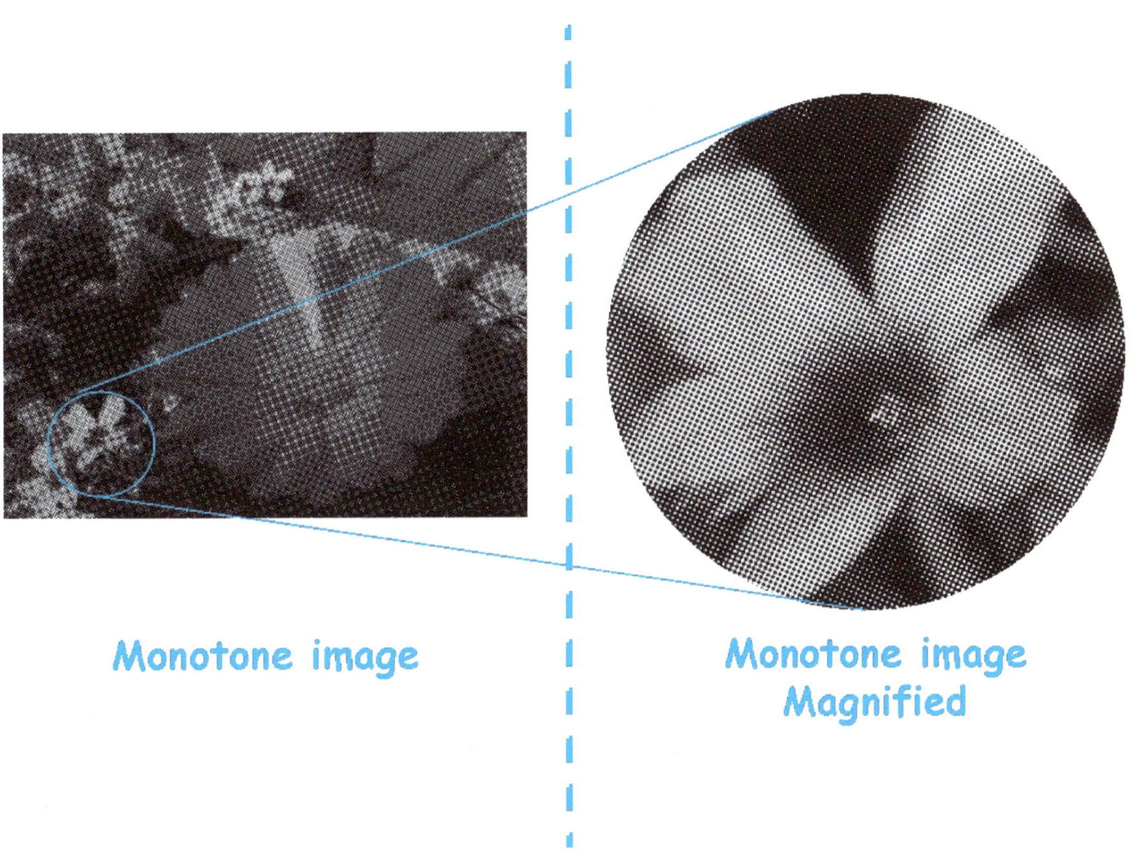

Illustration 15. Notice the dots in the magnified part of the image.

So, you've got a design that glows, leaps off the screen, and is better than inventing sliced bread. Is anyone checking to understand how it will look after print? The issue is not so much the choice of colour but more so the size of the coloured graphics. Take a look at Illustration 16 below. Then review Illustration 3 above. From Illustration 3, we now see that the light colour has been gripped under the dark colour. Remember that this avoids unwanted white gaps if we tuck the lighter colour under the darker colour. In Illustration 16, we can easily see that the large block of purple is big enough for it to be gripped so that the purple colour remains true. However, the text is much smaller, and so even the smallest grip / trap floods the entire area behind the text. The purple text is said to be overprinting. Take a look at the three circles and notice that the purple text has been tainted by the orange and now appears much darker. To test how this appears is to use the darken or multiply mode in Adobe Illustrator® if this is your program of choice. Other programs may have similar features that simulate print.

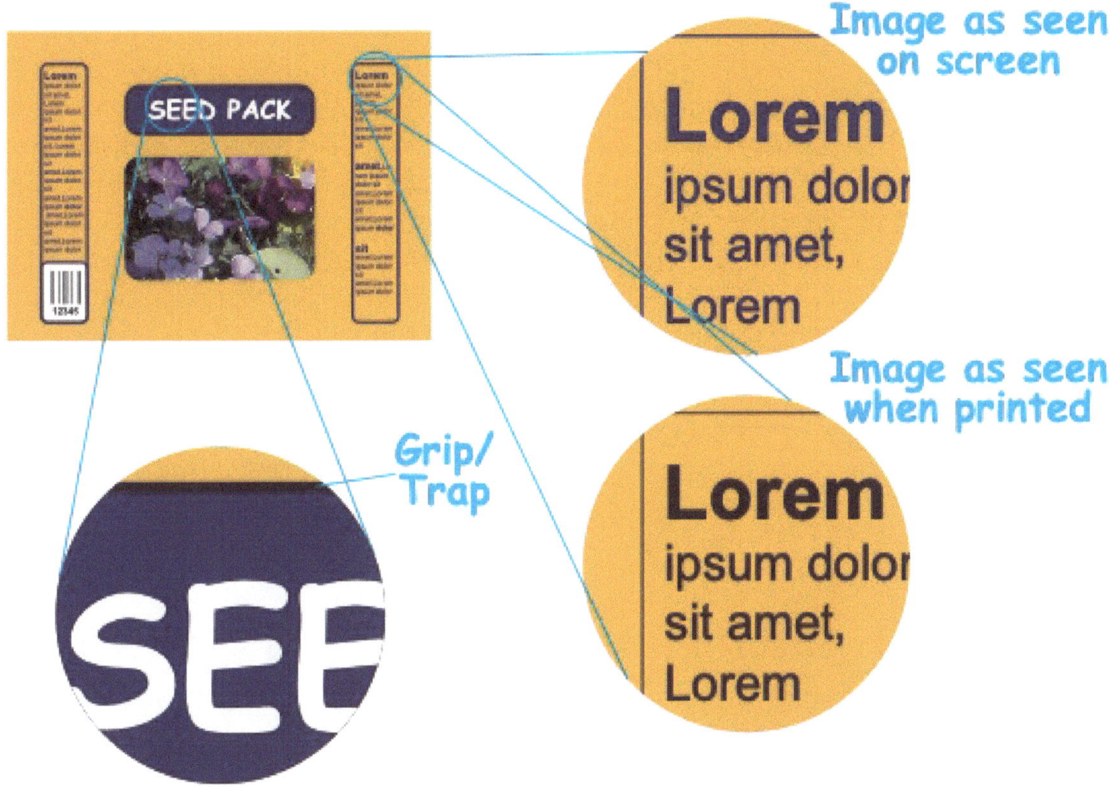

Illustration 16. Take note of how the colour shifts from what is seen on screen to what happens in print. The colour changes from a clean purple to a dirty purple.

🚫 **Issue**: Colour clash involving overprint is unavoidable due to an object or graphic size. This, when not picked up at design stage could cause concern about the final print colours and more specifically how they appear.

🏆 **Hot Tip**: Use the overprint 'flaw' as part of your design. Alternatively, you can use black or a much dark colour than the base colour. Another option is to use a colour that won't conflict. An example of this is green text on a yellow background. Finally, a fourth option is to use white text, providing it's big enough as discussed in the previous section. Also, is it a high enough contrast against the background to be legible?

How design impacts production cost:

Every designer should be savvy about the end cost of every design. A customer who knows that you have taken the time to understand their cost is a much more appreciative customer. Every design has a production cost attached to it. This is why, quite often, a design is signed off by a customer, and the final printed job looks quite different. It is because the cost of producing the design(s) had become restrictive. Most of the time, for a one-off design, the cost does not shift greatly with most changes needed or could double. However, for a range or series of products, the production cost can rocket. This can then be reflected in the design changes requested by your client at the production house. Review Illustrations 17 & 18 below.

A: 5 colour print
Colours are CMYK + Pantone® Purple 255

B: 5 colour print
Colours are CMYK + Pantone® Purple 255

C: 5 colour print
Colours are CMYK + Pantone® Purple 255

Illustration 17. Study the three images above and think about cost impact of each design choice in the three situations following: Then analyse the cost sheet below.

Table of Production Cost

SINGLE DESIGN	DESIGN A number of plates	DESIGN B number of plates	DESIGN C number of plates
First run of the design	5	5	5
A text change to the back of pack	1	4	1
Total Plates	6	9	6

RANGE OF DESIGNS	DESIGN A number of plates	DESIGN B number of plates	DESIGN C number of plates
Design 1	5	5	5
Design 2	2	5	2
Design 3	2	5	2
Design 4	2	5	2
Design 5	2	5	2
Design 6	2	5	2
Design 7	2	5	2
Design 8	2	5	2
Design 9	2	5	2
Design 10	2	5	2
Total number of plates across the range for the first run	23	50	23
A text change to the back of pack	10	40	10
Total Plates	33	90	33

Illustration 18. How production cost is impacted by design decisions.

For a stand-alone design A, the initial cost is for five plates. Should we need to have a text change as simple as removing one letter, the cost is for one plate as the text is on the black plate. Only the black plate will be replaced. Review Illustration 1 again.

For a stand-alone design B, the initial cost is for five plates. Should we need to have a text change as simple as removing one letter, the cost is for four plates as the text is being 'cut out' of the multi-coloured CMYK background. The text is a negative space text, as discussed in the previous sections. Review Illustration 12.

For a stand-alone design C, the initial cost is for five plates. Should we need to have a text change as simple as removing one letter, the cost is for one plate as the text is on the purple plate. Only the purple plate will be replaced. See Illustration 1 if unsure.

For a range of ten varieties using design A, the initial cost is for twenty-three plates. This is because there are three plates that are common or the same between each variant. These are the CMY. Only the black and the main title plates changes. Should we need to have a text change as simple as removing one letter, the cost is for ten plates for the range. This is because the text is on the black plate. Only the black plates will be replaced.

For a range of ten varieties using design B, the initial cost is for fifty plates. This is because all five plates must be changed for each variant. Should we need to have a text change as simple as removing one letter, the cost is for forty plates for the range. This is because the text has been cut out of four colours (CMYK).

For a range of ten varieties using design C, the initial cost is for twenty-three plates. This is because there are three plates that are common or the same between each variant. These are the CMY. Only the black and the main title plates change. Should we need to have a text change as simple as removing one letter, the cost is for ten plates for the range. This is because the text is on the purple plate. Only the purple plate will be replaced.

Other associated costs: Everything has a cost in any commercial operation. This means that there are associated costs for each plate mounted to the press. The higher the number of plates, the higher the cost of mounting, dismounting, and setting in the press. Designs A and B are similar so we can say that the three common plates are set up in the press; for each other variant, the cost is two additional set-ups. So, it is set-up cost x23. However, for design B, a full set of plates must be set to the press for each variant. So, it is set-up cost x50.

We can see how tweaking a design can reduce production costs. This is not to say that every design must be the same. If a designer considers the design carefully, they can plan for the customer's budget as it relates to plate and associated production cost.

Strip lamination:

Strip lamination allows a client to print on paper with its craft feel while creating a product view window. The same effect can be recreated with a film and white ink to block out the non-window areas, but film does not have the same tactility as paper. To achieve a similar effect a tactile varnish must be used. This type of strip lamination package can often be seen in use for sausages, fruit, and bread, to name a few.

Example of Strip Lamination

Illustration 19 shows an arrangement to use a transparent window through which the product can be viewed. This is achieved with two materials. A clear film onto which paper is laminated. This is different to a printed window in which there is an area free from print so as to view the product.

Ⓢ **Issue**: 1. Printing on the window area. 2. Shape of the window area.

🏆 **Hot Tip**: Printing on the window area for strip lamination should be avoided for two reasons. The first is the change in the colours of the design. Let us suppose, for example, that we wanted to print part of the above floral design to continue onto the window area. There will be a difference in colours as paper and film are two distinct substrates. If there is print on the window, it should be a distinct part of the design, not using the same imagery of the paper-printed areas that need to match.

Avoid the design shape flowing from the paper-printed area into the window. The window shape using current technology is restricted to two vertical lines of paper on the window borders.

Common design situations:
How to save the print day and retain control of the design

Barcode size and placement:

🚫 **Issues**: Avoid using coloured backgrounds, sizes below 85%.

🏆 **Hot Tip**: Keep barcodes to a maximum reduction of 85% of the program creation size (100%). Background colours or images can interfere with scan-ability. No store wants to stock a product that slows down production, i.e., items passing the till. On shrink wraps; barcodes should have horizontal bars. They should also occur at the area of the product with the least possibility of shrink. That is to say the widest part of the product with the least curve or embellishment.

Colour modes:

🚫 **Issues**: Avoid RGB colour mode for images or print colours.

🏆 **Hot Tip**: Printers never use RGB colours. All RGB images supplied will be changed. This means all artwork will be converted to CMYK and or spot Pantone® colours. The issue is that RGB has a wider gamut (range) of colour that can be created with CYMK combinations. They are also more intense on-screen. Because print systems used CMYK, the image must be converted, and very often, the most noticeable change is a darkening and loss of intensity of colour. Convert colours and adjust in studio to maintain maximum control of the print outcome.

Ink Colours:

🚫 **Issues**: Too many or non-cohesive colours.

🏆 **Hot Tip**: Check separations and ensure that the only colours in the supplied file are equal to or lower than the number of colours of the printing press. This must include any printed special effects. Also, ensure that all colours that appear as the same are coloured the same, e.g., a light green that is meant to be the same,

should be made up of exactly the same process ink combination. Use Pantone®
where possible and keep these consistent.

Importance of white ink:

🚫 **Issues**: White ink not accounted for.

🏆 **Hot Tip**: Ninety-seven percent of designs will require a white plate. Account
for this in your colour count. Note: if not printed on a white substrate it will require
white ink. Also note that some white substrates require white ink e.g. grease proof
paper.

Combining large solid print with small text:

🚫 **Issues**: Avoid using large solid areas and text below 20 points on the same
plate, for much of the same reason as for white mentioned above.

🏆 **Hot Tip**: Split the colours and run two of the same ink colours or consider
switching the printed text colour to a plate without large solid areas.

File supply:

🚫 **Issues**: Avoid random file formats.

🏆 **Hot Tip**: Supply files for line work as press-ready PDF, Adobe illustrator®, or
EPS formats. If you have another program aside from Adobe Illustrator, save / save
as or export your file to PDF or EPS. For image work, supply as high-resolution
300DPI or above Photoshop® (.psd), TIFF, or JPG / JPEG. When the image is
embedded always still include your high resolution files as separate archives.

Gradients to white:

🚫 **Issues**: Avoid running gradients to white.

🏆 **Hot Tip**: Gravure, offset litho, and digital can comfortably print your gradient to white. Flexo tends to print to a minimum of two percent of a colour. This means that if your gradient has CMYK at the darkest area, then the whites will have two percent of each of the CMYK colours. This makes the white areas appear dirty as compared to the other three print methods mentioned above. Solution one: use fewer colours in the darkest area so that the lighter areas are cleaner. Solution two: use a single spot colour to create the gradient. With this option, the printer can vary the print process for the best result possible.

Image resolutions:

🚫 **Issues**: Poor-quality images result in poor-quality prints.

🏆 **Hot Tip**: Supply images at 100% of the printed size required or larger. For JPEG, supply at 300DPI and a minimum of 200% of the size required. JPEGs at 200% will give better results. TIFF and PSD files can be supplied at a minimum of 100% of the size required, a minimum of 300DPI.

Metallic substrate:

🚫 **Issues**: Not creating your white plate/ image.

🏆 **Hot Tip**: Enquire if your package or label is going to use metallic film. Metallic papers often aid in marketing or in the case of film specification increases shelf life and reduces spoilage, e.g., potato chips / crisps. Here is a chance to jazz up the design and take advantage of the metallic background. For labels, metallic papers may be more expensive, but they do pack a punch in selling power. Create or indicate the areas that you want as metallic.

New flashes:

🚫 **Issues**: New, improved, 200% more, vegan flashes impact the cost of the succeeding design. Review the section titled *How design impacts production cost*.

🏆 **Hot Tip**: Many companies use a design element (a flash) to announce a new size, shape, price, product, or flavour. Very often, these are positioned so that they, unfortunately, have the maximum negative dollar value impact on the cost of the next version. Investigate the cost of new plates affected by the placement of the flash.

Overprint areas:

🚫 **Issues**: Inks and varnishes appearing in the background of overprint areas.

🏆 **Hot Tip**: Keep these areas free or inks and varnishes. White where possible or extremely light colours. Keep in mind that on screen is not print. Think of the printed final printed result first.

Substrates and their importance to colour:

🚫 **Issues**: Understanding the effect of substrates and in particular laminates to colour.

🏆 **Hot Tip**: When it comes to laminates it is critical to understand the effect of transparent laminates on print. For example, reverse printing a transparent film then laminating behind the print gives better results than laminating on top of the ink. This is because the glue used can shift the colour slightly. This appears as a slightly grey cast to the image. Although this shift in colour is very minor, this can be planned for by choosing shades of colour that may negate this effect. Also, every substrate chosen can shift the colour simply because of the properties of the substrate itself. This is why colour is only measured within ranges and not a specific point. With recent developments in colour calibration the widths of these ranges are ever smaller.

Substrates: Understanding the choice: with matt film

🚫 **Issues**: Understanding the effect of matt substrates on colour.

Hot Tip: Matt substrates will matt or dullen the colours that they are printed to. Where a matt and gloss effects are required, it is best to print a gloss substrate and add a matt varnish. Note this reduces the number of printed colours that are available to print. It is possible to run a job through the press a second time to add a varnish however this will significant cost as well.

Tandem Prints

Issues: Customers often want to print two or more jobs together in tandem to control print cost, but the designer was not involved in the decision.

Hot Tip: Discuss tandem prints with customer before final artwork signoff. The combined number of colours and varnished should not exceed the number of print stations of the selected printer.

Using tints of solid colours:

Issues: Avoid using large solid areas of print with tints of the solid colour. This is very much the same reason as for white text printed on clear film mentioned above. Recall that although the tint appears solid on screen, it will actually be made up of dots. These dots may appear over-inked or over-impressed, as with the white on clear film example below.

Hot Tip: If you are using CMYK colours with your Pantone® colour in the design, recreate the solid colour tint from the CYMY inks. Alternatively, select a Pantone® ink that best represents the tint that you are trying to achieve from the darker colour.

White text printed on clear film:

Issues: On a clear film, there needs to be a strong lay-down of white ink (coat weight). White standard text (sans serif) below 20 point may appear over-impressed (too much plate pressure) or over-inked (too much ink lay-down), or both.

Selected specialised terminology:
Critical terminology for flexographic and other printing systems

Blind embossing: embossing: debossing: Images created by pressing paper and other materials into relief. These images can be raised, recessed, or a combination of both.

Colourway: The number of colours in a printed design.

Crimp seal: The seal formed by heating and pressing two materials to form a permanent bond. Usually seen on most plastic packaging.

Cromalin®: A close representation of the final print. Often used as a generic term. Replaced now by ORIS® and GMG® systems created on calibrated inkjet printers.

Crop marks: Printed lines showing where to trim a printed sheet. Note: Not required for jobs printed on a roll.

Densitometer: An electronic device that measures the density of printing inks.

Dot gain / Dot growth: The increase in size of the halftone dots due to the pressure required to transfer inks to substrate.

Draw-down: Sample of ink on substrate to check colours prior to print.

Duotone: Image made up of two coloured halftones.

Eye-mark / eye block: This is printed on the pack and triggers the packing machine's electronic eye to seal and cut the pack. This is usually seen as a black rectangle.

Eye-mark / eye block track: This is typically free of print. If in doubt, leave free of print. This can at times have print if it is a continuous print, i.e., there is no set pack length, therefore, no eye-mark. Or if the eye-mark is reversed, i.e., it is white.

Flood: To cover a printed page with ink, varnish, or plastic coating.

Highlight dot: The lightest halftone dots, e.g., two percent, typically below twenty percent.

Loupe: A magnifying glass used to review a printed image, plate, and position film.

Middle tones: The tones in a photograph that are approximately half as dark as the shadow area.

Midtone dot: The middle halftone dots, e.g., around fifty percent.

Monotone: Image made up of a single colour halftone.

Pre-press: The work carried out to prepare a graphic file for print, e.g., trapping, colour correction, plate-making.

Process printing: printing halftones using two or more of the CMYK colours.

Repeat: Where the pack is cut after being filled and sealed. Sealing and cutting is typically one operation.

Reverse printing: Printing on the underside of a substrate. Typically, this is done on transparent film to protect the ink from scratching off. For food products, there is usually a second film added behind the inked side. Minimal amount of print on the glue side of labels.

Separation (s): Describes the colour make-up of a piece of artwork typically on screen. Adobe Illustrator® shows this in the separations preview tab.

Shadow dot: The darkest halftone dots, e.g., eighty percent.

Slits: Where the pack is trimmed to its width on the press or in a separate operation.

Spectrophotometer: A specialised instrument for measuring brightness and colour by measuring the reflected wavelength of the colours being examined.

Substrate / material: This is printed on and used as a communication tool.

Tritone: Image made up of three colour halftones.

Web: This is the entire width of the material / substrate running through the printing press. Or the pack size x the number of packs across the press + any excess material / substrate

Reference: Flexible packaging artwork
Flexible packaging fast overview. Also see reference 1A-1C

Cutter - Illustrates perimeter of packaging / fold area / cut area / tear area / glue area

Overall measurements (part of cutter) of flattened bag / flow wrap / pouch / sachet

Overall measurement breakdown (part of the cutter) - To understand how the final package will fold

Bleed off - Where print touches the cutter extends a minimum of 2-10mm outside the cutter

Eye-mark - Triggers packaging equipment to seal and cut package. *not required for continuous wrap that is manually / Machine cut.

Eye-mark track – Print-free zone in which the eye-mark sits (eye-mark may be reversed)

Colour breakdown in legend - Printed Pantone® spot and process

Representations of spot, overall varnishes, windows, and special effects

Overprint areas - Should be free from varnish

Reference 1A: Flexible packaging cutter / keyline.

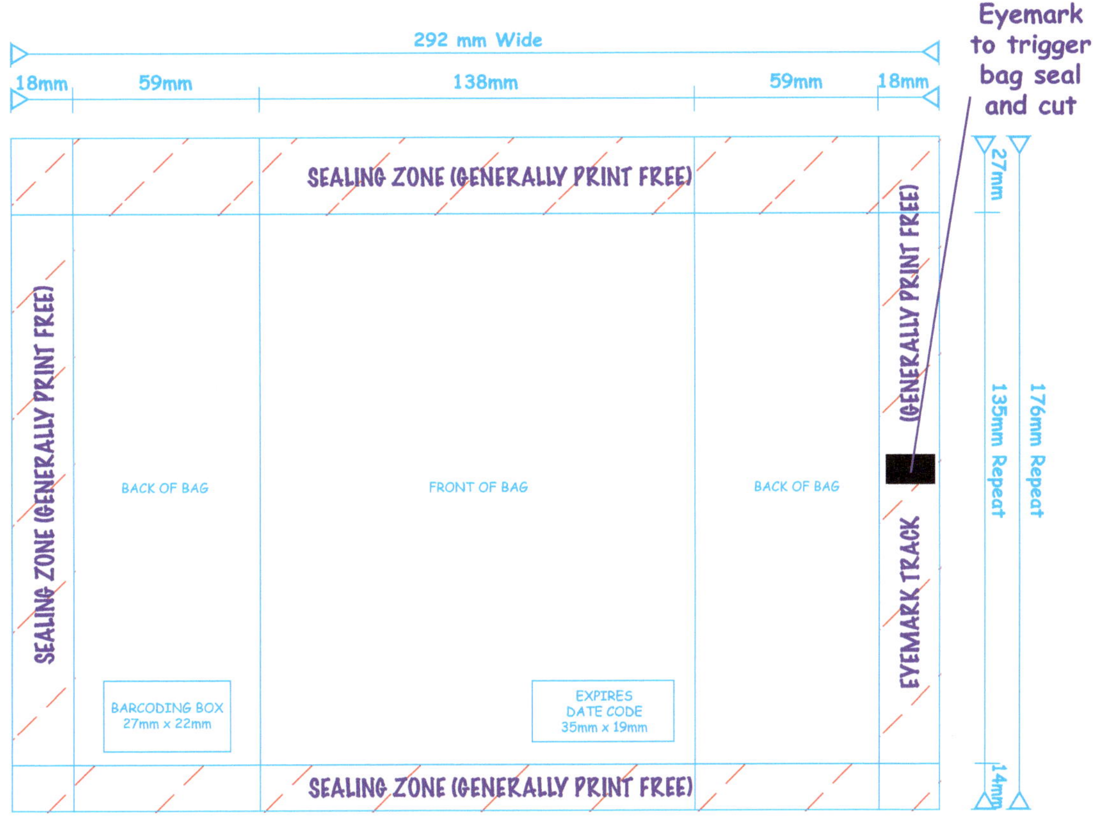

Reference 1B: Flexible packaging cutter / keyline with artwork underlay.

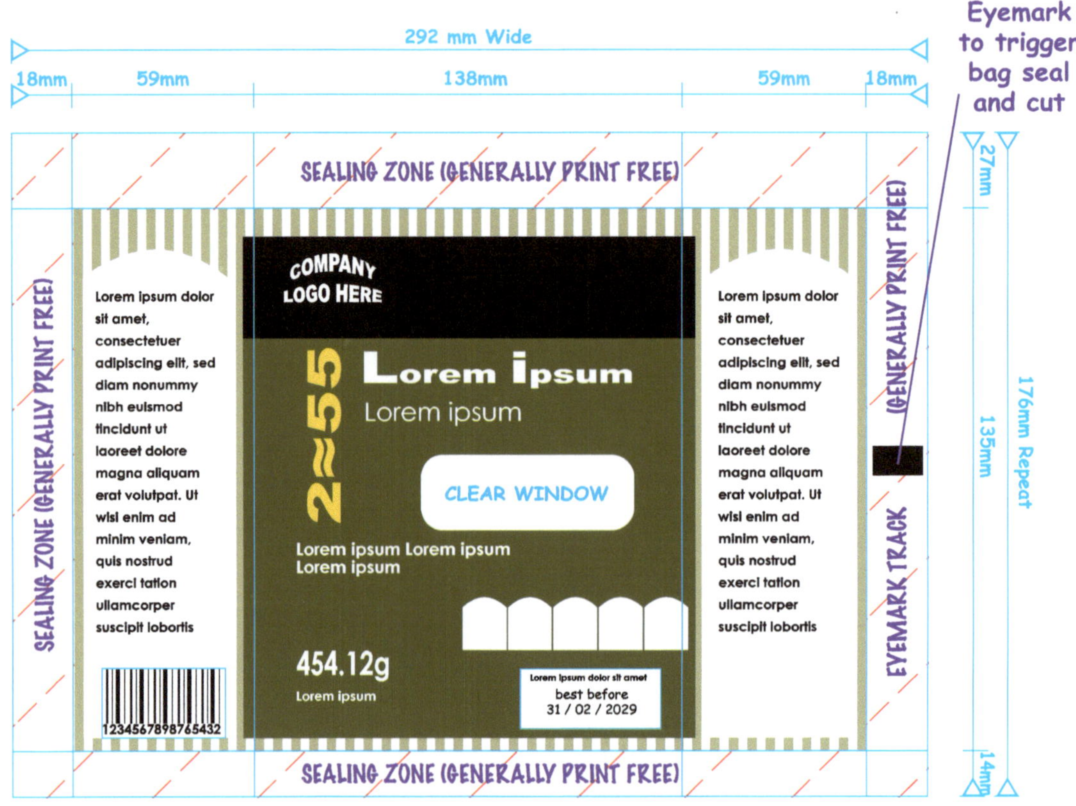

Reference 1C: Flexible packaging wrapped with window to view product.

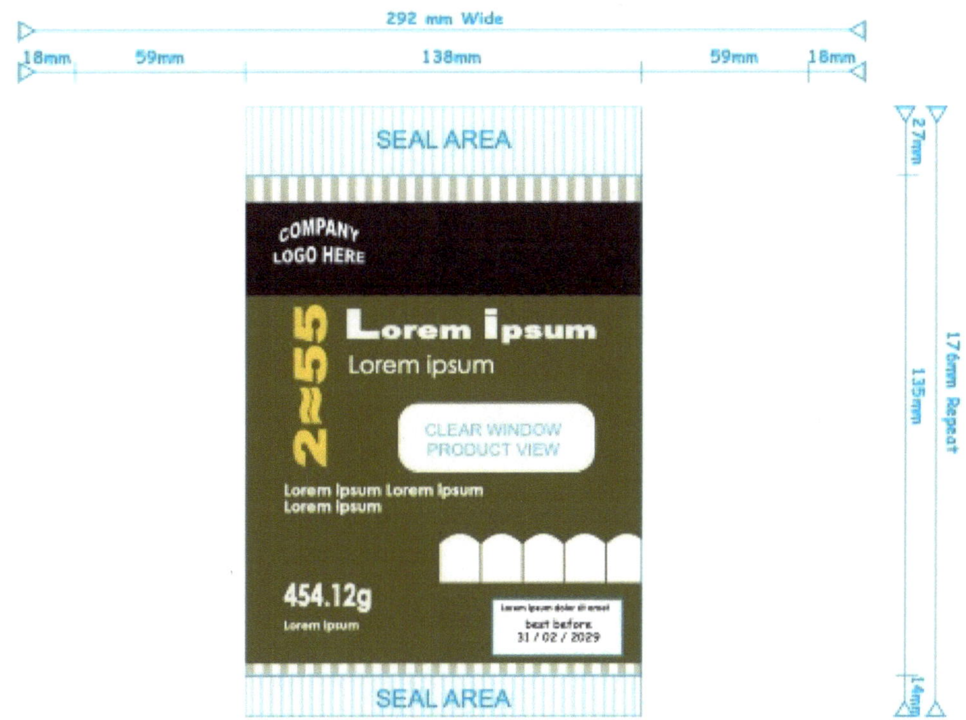

Reference: Label artwork
Labels fast overview. Also see reference 2A-2C

Cutter - Standard or special shape - illustrates the perimeter of the label. May also indicate tear strips and tamper-evident areas where applicable

Bleed off - Where print touches the cutter; it should extend 2-3mm outside the cutter

Colour breakdown in legend - Pantone® spot and process colours

Representations of spot/overall varnishes, embossing, hot foils, temperature, and light-sensitive security print

Reference 2A: Label die / cutter / keyline.

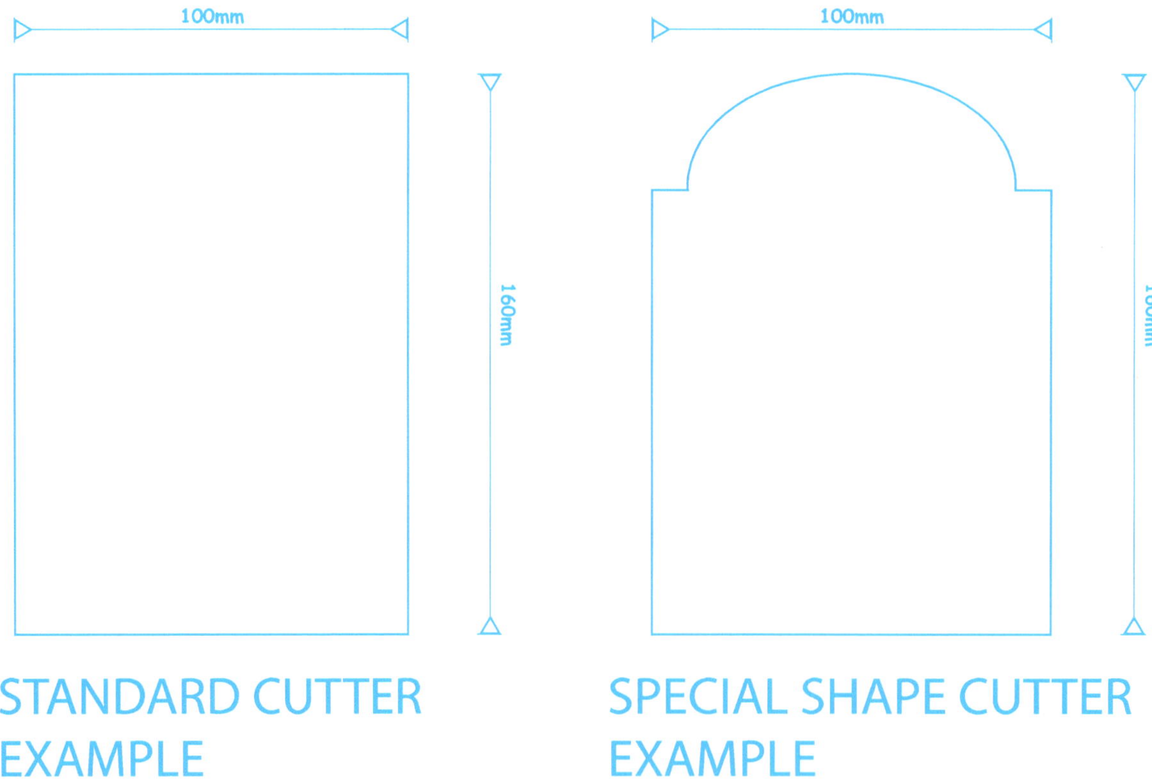

Reference 2B: Label cutter / keyline with artwork underlay.

STANDARD CUTTER EXAMPLE

SPECIAL SHAPE CUTTER EXAMPLE

Reference: Box / carton artwork
Board / carton packaging fast overview. Also see reference 3A-3C

Cutter - Perimeter of box / carton / fold / crease / tear / glue area

Bleed off (where image touches cutter)

Colour breakdown in legend - Pantone® spot and process colours

Representations of spot/overall varnishes, embossing, hot foils, temperature, and light-sensitive security print

Glue areas (image free and varnish free)

Reference 3A: Basic box / carton cutter / keyline.

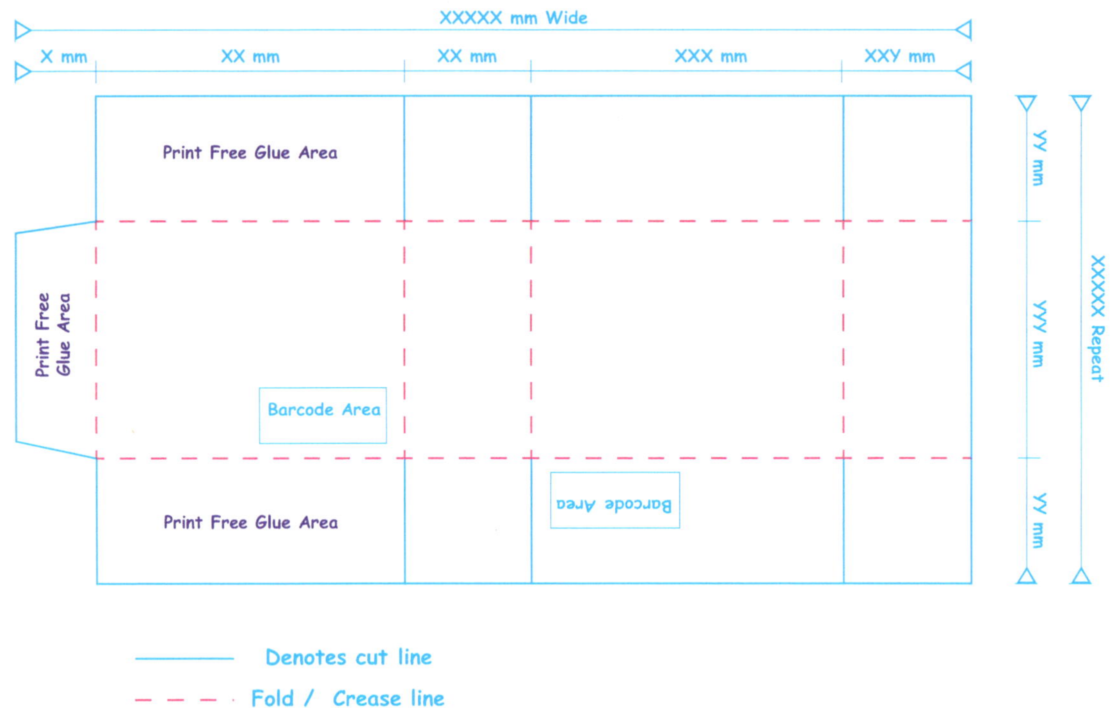

Reference 3B: Carton cutter / keyline with artwork underlay.

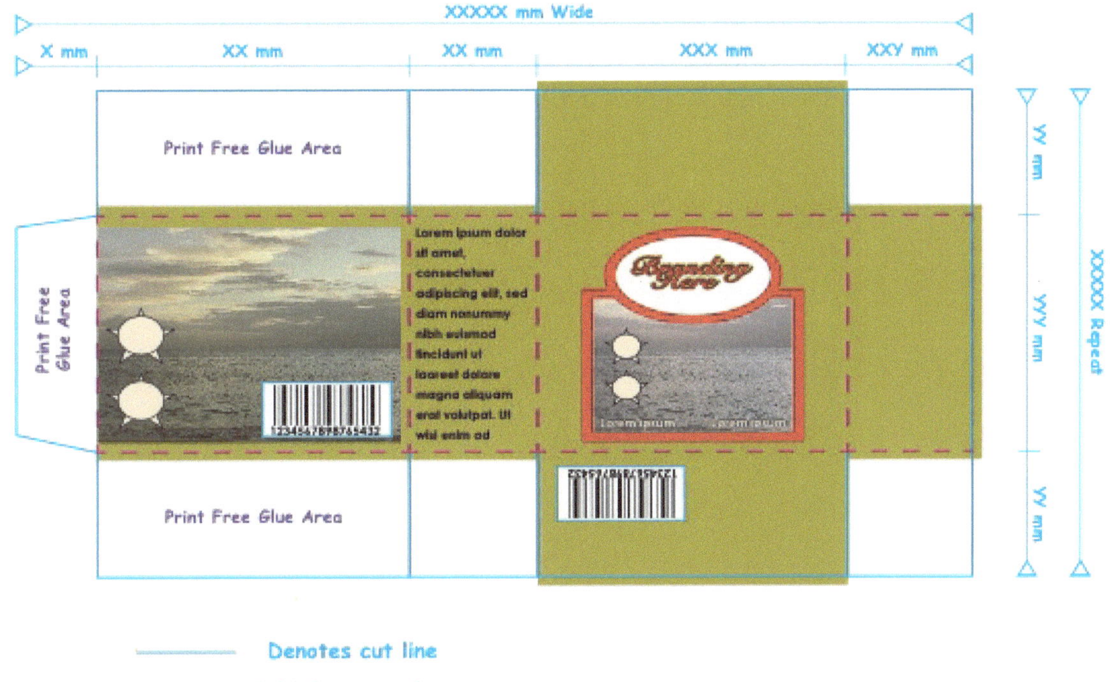

Reference 3C: Carton 2D views.

TOP VIEW
of box

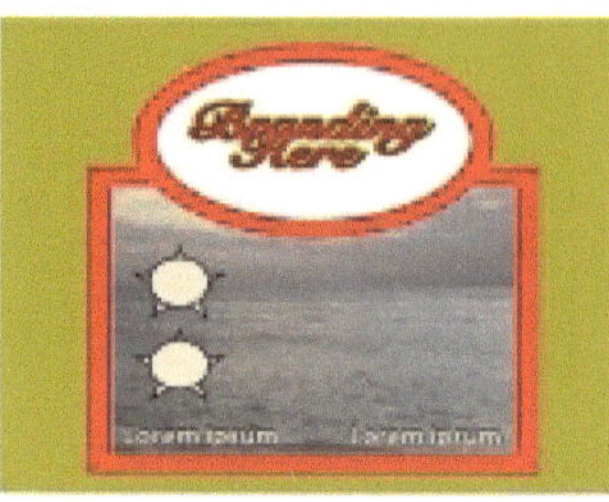

BACK VIEW
of box

SIDE VIEW
of box

FRONT VIEW
of box

SIDE VIEW
of box

BOTTOM VIEW
of box

If in reading this book you find that there is missing or incorrect information or a citation or quote missing; please do contact me with the details and I will make the appropriate corrections where needed.

 The views and opinions are "those of the authors and do not necessarily reflect the official policy or position of any other agency, organization, employer or company